Learning the Animal Alphabet A to Z

Written and Illustrated
by
Rebecca B. Pinckney

Copyright © 2023 by Rebecca B. Pinckney

All rights reserved. No part of this book may be reproduced or transmitted in any form or by any means, electronic or mechanical, including photocopy, recording, or information storage and retrieval systems, without permission in writing from the publisher. For permission requests, solicit the publisher via the address below.

Learning the Animal Alphabet - A to Z
By Rebecca Pinckney
RebeccaPinckney.com

ISBN 978-1-954000-56-8 (Hardback)
ISBN 978-1-954000-57-5 (eBook)

Editor: Bernadette Eastland
Cover design lead: Teresa Evans
Interior design: Teresa Evans

Published 2023, by Publish Authority
300 Colonial Center Parkway, Suite 100
Roswell, GA 30076-4892 USA
PublishAuthority.com

Printed in the United States of America
First edition

Chase, Lyda, Iris, Vance, Heidi, and Aubrey

In this book are 26 animals to see.
Each beginning letter teaches the ABCs.

"O Lord, how manifold are Your works!
In wisdom you have made them all.
Living things both great and small."
Adapted from Psalms – 104:25-26 ESV

Anteater

    Anteaters eat ants, termites, fruit, and other small animals.

    There are no teeth in their mouths, but they use their long sticky tongues to lap up insects.

    Their two front legs have claws that turn under when they walk.

    Some anteaters are as small as squirrels, others are as large as a twenty-five-pound dog.

The letter "A" has three different sounds:
    "ă" - as in tap
    "ā" - as in name
    "ä" - as in a-ha.

"A" is for anteater, whose tongue can catch its dinner.

Bear

Bears are very smart mammals.

They have excellent senses of smell, sight, and hearing.

In cold climates they go into a deep sleep called hibernation.

They can walk short distances on their hind legs and can easily climb trees.

The letter "B" sounds like:
"b" - as in bat.

"B" is for bear who sleeps through the winter.

Crocodile

A crocodile is a large cold-blooded reptile that hatches from an egg.

They are dark green in color with scaly skin.

They eat fish, amphibians, birds, mammals, and other reptiles.

During their lifetime they wear out up to 4,000 teeth.

A crocodile's snout is shaped like a pointed "V" and an alligator's snout is shaped like a rounded "U".

The letter "C" has two sounds:
 "c" as in crocodile
 "k" as in cop.

"C" is for crocodile with teeth big and white.

Deer

Male deer are called bucks and wear a rack of antlers on their heads.

Female deer are called does, and baby deer are called fawns.

These animals can run up to thirty miles an hour. They are good swimmers. They can hear and smell very well.

There is a type of deer that will bounce up and down on their feet when they are scared.

This action is called stotting.

The letter "D" sounds like:
   "d" as in dog.

"D" is for deer who runs away in fright.

Egret

The egret is a bird that lives on all continents in the world except Australia.

They are completely white with a yellow beak and gray legs.

You will always find them living together in groups.

The National Audubon Society has a picture of the egret as its symbol.

"E" has two sounds:
  "ĕ" - as in egg
  "ē" - as in eagle.

"E" is for egret fishing near the sea.

Frog

Frogs are cold-blooded reptiles that hatch from eggs.

There are thousands of different types of frogs all over the world.

The biggest is called Goliath, and the smallest is known as "Mimi mum".

Some frogs can jump up to twenty times their body length.

Frogs drink water through their skin.

The letter "F" sounds like:
"f" - as in family.

"F" is for frog hopping past so freely.

Goose

The female bird is called a goose, the male is called a gander, and the newborn is called a gosling.

They live in the wild and are also tame.

When a gosling hatches it will bond or "imprint" to whatever animal it first sees.

A goose and a gander mate for life and nest in the same spot every year.

"G" has two sounds:
 "g" - as in goat
 "j" - as in giraffe.

"G" is for goose sitting on a nest.

It is one of the most intelligent birds and is a good watch animal for it honks at strangers.

Hedgehog

A hedgehog is a nocturnal mammal that moves around only at night.

The "hedge" part of their name comes from the nests they build near the hedges.

The "hog" part comes from the small grunting or snorting sounds they make similar to a pig.

They have over 7,000 spines on their hides.

Gardeners appreciate hedgehogs because they eat beetles, caterpillars, and other pests that attack garden plants.

The letter "H" sounds like:
  "h" - as in happy.

"H" is for hedgehog waddling through the grass.

Ibis

These graceful birds with a long-curved beak have lived for centuries.

Their bill is used to probe into water or mud for food.

The food they eat includes beetles, fish, insects, small plants, shellfish, and reptiles.

They live in warm areas of the world near the equator.

The letter "I" has three sounds:
- "ĭ" - as in igloo
- "ī" - as in ice
- "ē" - as in ski.

"Couples are most likely to nest in trees with two or three other ibis couples."

"I" is for ibis walking in the rain.

Jaguar

This animal is in the cat family and is highly endangered.

That means there are very few of them left in the wild.

It is about six feet long and weighs eighty pounds

It lives in the Amazon and the tropical wetlands of South America and they are excellent swimmers.

Its coat has brown rose shaped marks with a black dot in the middle.

The letter "J" sounds like:
"j" as in jeep.

"J" is for jaguar stalking on the plain.

Kiwi

The kiwi bird is nocturnal and is about the size of a large chicken.

Their short brown feathers look like fur and their whiskers look like those on a cat.

It is the only bird with nostrils at the end of its beak.

Their eyesight is weak but their senses of smell, hearing, and touch are very strong.

The letter "k" sounds like:
"k" - as in keep.

"K" is for kiwi a very shy bird, you see.

Lion

Lions are the only cats that live in a group called a pride.

Female lions are the main hunters.

Their roar can be heard up to five miles.

They pee around their territory to keep out other lions who may come into their land and take their food

The letter "L" sounds like:
   "l" - as in look.

"L" is for lion. His roar doesn't scare me!

Mouse

A mouse is a good jumper, climber, and swimmer.

They produce forty to one-hundred droppings a day.

They can squeeze through the tiniest gap.

Their teeth never stop growing so they chew constantly.

The letter "M" sounds like:
"m" - as in man.

"M" is for mouse hiding near the door.

Nightingale

This bird can sing over one-thousand different songs.

Scientists think they can do this because their brains are bigger than most other birds.

They live in open forests or thickets and fly at the speeds of up to eighteen miles per hour.

The Letter "N" sounds like:
   "n" - as in nest.

"N" is for nightingale singing loud and sure.

Octopus

An octopus is an ocean creature known as mollusks.

It has no skeleton or spine and each of its eight legs operate by its own brain.

They are very smart and their blood is blue.

To escape its enemies it squirts out a cloud of black ink.

The Letter "O" has three sounds:
  "ŏ" - as in odd
  "ō" - as in oven
  "ö" - as in lemon.

"O" is for octopus swimming in a pool.

Pelican

Pelicans are among the largest flying birds.

Some pelicans have a wingspan more than six and a half feet wide.

Their huge throat pouch can hold up to three gallons of water.

They are excellent fliers and can soar like an eagle.

The letter "P" sounds like:
 "P" - as in pig.

"P" is for pelican catching a school of fish.

Quail

Quail are called game birds and live alone usually, but they form flocks in the fall.

A female can lay ten to twenty eggs at one time.

Quail wings are short, it can fly only a few feet.

Their diet consists of seeds, grains, and insects.

"Q" has two sounds:
    "q" - as in queen
    "k" - as in bouquet.

"Q" is for quail flying just a short way.

Rooster

Roosters are male chickens whose role is to protect the flock.

In olden days a rooster was called a cockerel or a cock.

They have bright colored feathers, large combs on the tip of their head and a trademark crow.

They are very sociable and have a great memory for human faces.

The letter "R" sounds like "r" - as in rabbit.

"R" is for rooster crowing in the new day.

Sheep

Sheep are smart and like to live in groups.

The iris part of a sheep's eye is square which allows them to see all around their head.

Their wool, milk, and meat make them useful to people.

A male sheep is called a ram, the female an ewe, and the baby a lambkin.

The Letter "S" has two sounds:
- "s" - as in sat
- "z" - as in rubs.

A mother ewe can recognize their lambkin's bleat.

"S" is for sheep. Its habits are meek and quiet.

Turkey

Turkeys are wild and domesticated.

In the wild they are very smart and hard to catch.

Only the male turkey makes a gobbling sound.

They are prized for their meat and their feathers.

The letter "T" sounds like:
 "t" - as in time.

"T" is for turkey whose gobble makes a racket.

Unicorn Fish

The unicorn fish has a bony horn on the front of its head.

This flat, oval fish grows up to two feet long and is a gray-blue color.

The Indian Ocean and the reefs around Hawaii are its home.

It has the amazing ability to change color depending on where it swims.

The letter "U" sounds like:
 "ŭ" - as in fun
 "ū" - as in flu
 "ü" - as in build.

"U" is for a Unicorn Fish that has a horn on its head.

Vicuña

This swift graceful animal lives in the high mountains of South America and in the Andean region of Peru.

It is a cousin to the camel and is prized for producing some of the finest wool in the world. It is considered the smallest animal in the camel family.

When they are scared they emit a high squeaking sound.

The vicuña has the honor to be pictured on the crest of the Peruvian flag.

The letter "V" sounds like:
   "v" - as in valentine.

"V" is for vicuña traversing the mountain range.

Walrus

A walrus is very large, brown animal shaped like a torpedo and they live near the North Pole.

Their front and back feet are big flippers.

Two large white tusks grow out of their mouths which allow them to pull themselves along the shore.

Their mouths are lined with long, drooping whiskers and they love to make loud bellowing sounds.

The letter "W" sounds like:
 "w" - as in walrus.

"W" is for walrus whose tusks are big and curvy.

Xolo

    A Xolo is from the country of Mexico and it has no hair on its body.

    Its full name is Xoloitzcuinte which is pronounced "Zolo-its-squinty."

    They were bred as hunting dogs and like to travel in packs.

    They are friendly, affectionate, and even tempered.

The letter "X" has two sounds:
- "x" - as in fox
- "z" - as in xylophone

Yak

The yak is a pack animal that carries loads for people; it is in the cattle family.

They look like long-haired oxen with short legs and horns and have a distinctive hump on their backs.

Their home is in the highest mountains in the world up to the 2,000 feet range.

The people of Tibet use them for food and also use their fur to make tents, outer wear, ropes, and bags.

The letter "Y" has three sounds:
 "yuh" - as in syrup
 "ih" - as in candy
 "ī" as in bye-bye.

"Y" is for yak whose fur can be woven into a coat.

Zebra

The zebra is a member of the horse family.

It wears distinctive black and white stripes on its coat which help to camouflage it from its enemies.

It can run in large herds numbering in the thousands at speeds up to forty-five miles per hour.

A group of zebras is call a dazzle.

The letter "Z" has two sounds:
 "z" - as in zone
 "zh" - as in azure

"Z" is for zebra whose stripes are black and white.

This alphabet book has come to an end.
I hope you have enjoyed it and will read it again.

Learning the Animal Alphabet A to Z" was written to help a child learn to read.

Many writers have written about the reading process. We humans are not wired to learn to read. It doesn't just happen like walking or speaking. We have to work at it.

In the English language words consist of twenty-six symbols -- the alphabet. These symbols have roles and the reader has to know them all.

We 'hear' the sounds associated with the symbols to form a word. We have to decipher not only the word but a string of words -- a sentence which conveys a statement or a command or a question. Then we have to comprehend and retain what we have just read!

As an experienced Reading Specialist who taught in public and private schools, this book was written to assist the child to learn the letter sounds in the alphabet. In addition, I hope the reader will enjoy learning facts about each creature.

> Rebecca B. Pinckney, B.S., M.S., Ed.S. 5/10/2022

References

Dear Reader,
If a reference for an animal has gone away,
Keep searching,
on your own,
for one that is okay.
		Rebecca Pinckney, author.

Websites accessed April 24, 2023

Anteater:
https://facts.net/anteater-facts/
https://kids.britannica.com/kids/article/anteater/351396

Bear:
https://easyscienceforkids.com/all-about-bears/
https://onekindplanet.org/animal/black-bear/
https://facts.net/bear-facts/

Crocodile:
https://www.coolkidfacts.com/reptiles/ https://kids.kiddle.co/Crocodile#:~:text=A%20crocodile%20is%20a%20large,sleep%20out%20the%20dry%20season.
https://a-z-animals.com/blog/10-incredible-crocodile-facts/

Deer:
https://www.britannica.com/animal/mule-deer
https://kids.kiddle.co/Deer#:~:text=There%20are%20about%2060%20species,about%203%20to%205%20years.

Egret:
https://kids.britannica.com/students/article/egret/310607/media
https://kids.kiddle.co/Great_Egret
https://study.com/academy/lesson/egret-facts-lesson-for-kids.html

Frog:
https://kids.britannica.com/kids/article/frog/353154
https://easyscienceforkids.com/all-about-frogs-and-toads/

Goose:
https://justfunfacts.com/?s=geese
https://kids.nationalgeographic.com/animals/birds/facts/canada-goose
https://easyscienceforkids.com/all-about-geese/

Hedgehog:
https://www.lovethegarden.com/uk-en/article/15-hedgehog-facts-kids
https://www.coolfactsforkids.com/hedgehog-facts-for-kids/

Ibis:
https://kids.britannica.com/kids/article/ibis/390771
https://easyscienceforkids.com/ibis-facts/
https://www.allaboutbirds.org/guide/White_Ibis/

Jaguar:
https://www.sciencekids.co.nz/sciencefacts/animals/jaguar.html
https://kids.nationalgeographic.com/animals/mammals/facts/jaguar
https://www.wwf.org.uk/learn/fascinating-facts/jaguars

Kiwi Bird:
https://easyscienceforkids.com/all-about-kiwis/
https://facts.net/kiwi-bird-facts/

Lion:
https://www.wwf.org.uk/learn/fascinating-facts/lions
https://kids.nationalgeographic.com/animals/mammals/facts/lion
https://animalfactguide.com/animal-facts/lion/

Mouse:
https://www.pestworldforkids.org/pest-guide/mice/
https://www.sciencekids.co.nz/sciencefacts/animals/mouse.html
https://onekindplanet.org/animal/mouse/

Nightingale:
https://kids.kiddle.co/Nightingale
https://kids.britannica.com/kids/article/nightingale/390132
https://www.discoverwildlife.com/animal-facts/birds/facts-about-nightingale/

Octopus:
https://www.toucanbox.com/facts-for-kids/octopus-facts
https://smartclass4kids.com/science/animal-facts/octopus-facts/
https://kids.nationalgeographic.com/animals/invertebrates/facts/octopus

Pelican:
https://easyscienceforkids.com/?s=pelicans
https://justfunfacts.com/interesting-facts-about-pelicans/#:~:text=Many%20pelicans%20fish%20by%20swimming%20in%20cooperative%20groups.&text=When%20fish%20congregate%20in%20the,snares%20them%20in%20its%20bill.

Quail:
https://easyscienceforkids.com/all-about-quail/
https://kidskonnect.com/animals/quail/
https://quailforever.org/Habitat/Why-Habitat/Quail-Facts.aspx

Rooster:
https://switchzoo.com/profiles/rooster.htm
https://kidadl.com/facts/animals/rooster-facts
https://www.iamcountryside.com/backyard%20poultry

Sheep:
https://www.sciencekids.co.nz/sciencefacts/animals/sheep.html
https://kidadl.com/facts/animals/sheep-facts
https://www.coolkidfacts.com/facts-about-sheep/

Turkey:
https://www.worldanimalprotection.us/blogs/10-turkey-facts
https://www.coolfactsforkids.com/turkey-facts-for-kids/
https://kidadl.com/facts/animals/wild-turkey-facts

Unicorn Fish:
https://aqua.org/explore/animals/spotted-unicornfish
https://www.britannica.com/animal/unicorn-fish-Naso-genus
https://answersingenesis.org/kids/fish/unicornfish/

Vicuña:
https://animalia.bio/es/vicuna
https://justfunfacts.com/interesting-facts-about-vicunas/#:~:text=Vicunas%20have%20unique%20rodent%2Dlike,mammals%20of%20the%20same%20size.
https://kids.britannica.com/kids/article/vicu%C3%B1a/471260/media

Walrus:
https://kids.nationalgeographic.com/animals/mammals/facts/walrus
https://easyscienceforkids.com/all-about-walruses/
https://www.kidsplayandcreate.com/fun-walrus-facts-for-kids/

Xoloitzcintle:
https://www.akc.org/expert-advice/dog-breeds/10-facts-about-xoloitzcuintlis/
https://www.akc.org/dog-breeds/xoloitzcuintli/

Yak:
https://kids.britannica.com/kids/article/yak/390102
kidadl.com>animals>yak alphabetanimals.com/animal-dictionary/animals-that-start-with-y/yak

Zebra:
https://www.coolkidfacts.com/zebras-for-kids/
https://www.sciencekids.co.nz/sciencefacts/animals/zebra.html
https://kids.nationalgeographic.com/animals/mammals/facts/zebra

For more about the author, visit her website at

www.RebeccaPinckney.com

www.ingramcontent.com/pod-product-compliance
Lightning Source LLC
Chambersburg PA
CBHW061349010526
44107CB00011B/875